Themes from A Course in Miracles

HOW BROTHERS CAN GET ALONG

Editor, Merridy Cox

Lyrical Leaf
Publishing

Themes from A Course in Miracles: How Brothers Can Get Along

Editor © Merridy Cox Bradley, 2017

Photography © Merridy Cox Bradley, 2017

Author photo © Lisa Mininni Photographer, Toronto

Book Design: Shirley Aguinaldo

merridycox@gmail.com • http://LyricalLeaf.com

All quotes from *A Course in Miracles* are from the
First Edition, 2006, © Welcome Rain Publishers LLC.

Copyright of *A Course in Miracles* is now held by
Foundation for Inner Peace, P.O. Box 598, Mill Valley, 94942-0598
www.acim.org and info@acim.org.
With permission.

Library and Archives Canada Cataloguing in Publication

    Themes from A course in Miracles : how brothers can get along / editor, Merridy Cox.

Includes bibliographical references.
ISBN 978-0-9948481-2-3 (softcover)

    1. Course in Miracles. I. Bradley, Merridy Cox, editor

BP605.C68T54 2017   299'.93   C2016-908124-9

*L*yrical *L*eaf
Publishing

Themes from A Course in Miracles

HOW BROTHERS CAN GET ALONG

New Age books, such as *The Secret* and many others, refer to *A Course in Miracles*. Why is this course showing up as a source for so many authors? When a hard copy turned up in a second-hand bookshop, I decided to find out.

It turns out that *A Course in Miracles* was created by two American professors of medical psychology at Columbia University. Helen Schucman channeled the material and William Thetford recorded it. It took them seven years!

The channeled entity is Jesus Christ. The subject matter includes God the Father as Creator and the Holy Spirit as Teacher and Guide. In reading the *Course*, it is important to know that there is only *one* Son or Sonship. Every one of us and our brother is considered to be a Son of God or a vital part of the Son of God. The perception of a gap between our self and our brother is the problem that the Holy Spirit addresses. The miracle that closes the gap is forgiveness. We just need a little faith… God does the rest.

The *Course* is not an easy read. In fact, it is over 600 pages that often seem repetitive and circuitous. Nevertheless, I persevered and found many nuggets: concepts that are important in and of themselves and instructions for living in joy and harmony.

The *Course*, aside from the big book, includes a Workbook and a Manual for Teachers. Do students actually read the whole book? I wanted to see what I could glean from the book itself, and what I could share.

On each page of the book, I identified the most outstanding theme or concept and wrote it down. In this book, these themes have been arranged in order, page by page, under each chapter heading for easier reference. On occasion, two outstanding themes were found on a page. Note that the themes are not necessarily quotes but remain true to the concepts within the *Course*.

Original photographs, interspersed with the themes, illustrate real-life occupations and brothers in action.

Students of the *Course* will find this summary of themes useful for understanding. Some interesting discussions should come out of it.

Even if you do not follow New Age philosophy, read the themes to find out what the course is about and why it is the basis of so many modern spiritual teachings. Use the themes for comparison with your own beliefs.

— Merridy Cox, editor

Reference: *A Course in Miracles*. 2006. Welcome Rain Publishers LLC, original edition.

Contents

The Meaning of Miracles 1	Forgiveness and the Holy Relationship ... 49
The Separation and the Atonement 3	The Passing of the Dream 51
The Innocent Perception 5	The Attainment of Peace 55
The Illusions of the Ego 7	The Vision of Holiness 59
Healing and Wholeness 11	Reason and Perception 61
The Lessons of Love 13	Salvation and the Holy Relationship 65
The Gifts of the Kingdom 15	The War Against Yourself 67
The Journey Back 19	The Goal of Specialness 69
The Acceptance of the Atonement 23	The Justice of God 71
The Idols of Sickness 25	The Transition 73
God or the Ego 27	The Healing of the Dream 75
The Holy Spirit's Curriculum 29	The Undoing of Fear 79
The Guiltless World 33	The Awakening 81
Teaching for Truth 37	The New Beginning 83
The Holy Instant 41	The Final Vision 87
The Forgiveness of Illusions 47	Conclusion 91

CHAPTER 1
The Meaning of Miracles

The miracle is a sign of love among equals.

Miracles abolish time.

Miracles lead to revelation.

The means of Atonement is forgiving.

Miracles restore awareness of reality and a state of grace.

The Atonement unites all creations with their Creator.

Death does not exist;
reality belongs to the spirit.

The mind can elect what it chooses to serve.

A sense of separation from God is the only lack you need to correct.

You were created to create.

This is a course in mind training.

CHAPTER 2

The Separation and the Atonement

Because of your likeness to your Creator, you are creative.

Free will was given you for your joy.

The purpose of denial is to correct error.

Atonement can free you.

Atonement in physical terms is impossible.

All mistakes must be corrected at the level on which they occur.

The body is a learning device of the mind.

Egocentricity and fear occur together, unable to accept healing.

The miracle worker or healer accepts Atonement.

The miracle is an expression of charity and of Atonement, a sign of respect.

Your responsibility is correction of fear.

Conflict is an expression of fear.

The Atonement re-establishes the recognition of worth.

The power of your thoughts can move mountains.

The fundamental conflict in the world is creation vs. mis-creation.

God has only one Son; its oneness transcends the sum of its parts.

The length of the Last Judgment is shortened by miracles.

There is no reason to fear when everything you retain is lovable.
This is your part in the Atonement.

CHAPTER 3

The Innocent Perception

God does not believe in retribution.

The resurrection established the Atonement.

Innocence strives to protect its wholeness.

The Atonement radiates nothing but truth; it is the perfect lesson.

Innocence is not a partial attribute.

The Atonement (not sacrifice) is the only appropriate gift for God's altar.

Truth overcomes error.

Questioning illusions is the first step in undoing them. The miracle corrects them.

If you attack another, you will hurt yourself.

Right mindedness and right perception are miracle-minded.

All are called, but few choose to listen.

Pray for forgiveness and to be able to recognize what you already have.

Perception involves separation. Communion, not prayer, is the natural state of those who know.

Judgment involves rejection.

God offers words of mercy.

An authority problem is a denial of authorship.

Belief in separation and the Fall don't make them true.

Life and death are irreconcilable.

CHAPTER 4

The Illusions of the Ego

The result of genuine devotion is inspiration.

Learning and teaching change your mind.

Your worth is established by God.

Release yourself and release others.

Entrust your body and ego to God.

Become harmless and helpful.

Myths and magic have ego origins.

The Kingdom of Heaven is … you. The word *within* is unnecessary.

Ask for the gifts; God never fails to answer.

Prepare your mind for the Holy Spirit.

When you are not joyous, know that you have chosen wrongly.

Take opportunities to gladden yourself.

All things work together for good.

Meaningful seeking has a clear goal kept in mind.

Ask, what is the purpose? Then, decide.

Your mission is to live so as to demonstrate that you are not an ego.

Salvation is a collaborative venture.

Nothing real can be increased, except by sharing.

Be wholly helpful and wholly harmless.

CHAPTER 5

Healing and Wholeness

To heal is to make happy.

Healing is a thought by which two minds perceive their oneness and become glad.

The Holy Spirit will come only if you invite Him.

The Holy Spirit induces a kind of perception.

Healing is not creating; it is reparation.

When the ego was made, God placed in the mind the call to joy.

The Holy Spirit is your Guide in choosing;
He speaks for the right choice; He speaks for God.

Make the decision to share.

Share the Voice of the Holy Spirit to strengthen it.

You have no meaning, apart from your place in the Sonship.

The world is a teaching device.

Sharing is God's way of creating.

Give healing to hold it.

The Kingdom of Heaven in attained through the Atonement,
which releases you to create.

What you accept in your mind has reality for you.

The Holy Spirit, like the ego, is a decision.

What you want, you expect; your mind makes your future.

Vengeance cannot be shared; give it to the Holy Spirit who will undo it in you.

The Holy Spirit, who speaks for God in time, knows time to be meaningless.

There is no order of difficulty in miracles.

Recognize that you have actively decided wrongly but can as actively decide otherwise.

CHAPTER 6

The Lessons of Love

You are responsible for what you believe.

You are free to perceive yourself as persecuted or immune.

Resurrection is reawakening.

Resurrection is the symbol of sharing.

Develop your ability to be grateful.

Perceiving equality invites Atonement.

Find joy in a joyless place; you are not there.

The Holy Spirit is a bridge; everything meets in God.

For Atonement, recognize that the separation never occurred.

The Holy Spirit perceives every mind as one.

Remember that the Holy Spirit is the Answer, not the question.

When God created you, He made you part of Him.

You are a child of God.

God's Answer is your Teacher, the Holy Spirit.

The Holy Spirit shines away children's nightmares.

Those who communicate fear promote attack.

A teacher's goal is to strengthen motivation for change.

Allow the Holy Spirit to decide for God, for you.

The Holy Spirit sorts the true from the false in your mind.

Be consistent, despite chaos.

Having rests on giving, not on getting.

Vigilance against a sick mind is the way to heal it.

CHAPTER 7

The Gifts of the Kingdom

You have the power to add to the Kingdom.

To create like Him is to share His perfect Love.

To heal is to correct perception.

The Holy Spirit translates the laws of the Kingdom for you.

Only equals are at peace; be vigilant against competition.

The Holy Spirit must work through you; He is in you.

Seek the laws of truth; there is nothing else.

Healing is the one ability everyone can develop.

Fear does not gladden the unhealed healer.
Healing produces harmony.

The whole glory and perfect joy that is the Kingdom lies in you to give.

The mind that accepts attack cannot love.

Love is your power, which the ego must deny.

Your being is the knowledge of God;
the oneness of the Creator is your wholeness.

Your function is co-creator with God.

Withdraw your investment from your illusions.

Those who attack believe that they are deprived;
give them your blessing.

The Law of Sharing is to give something to keep it.

You can dispel the ego by withdrawing belief from it.

By accepting the Atonement, you are deciding against
the belief that you can be alone.

The Holy Spirit is in the part of the mind that lies between the ego and the spirit.

Unless you create, you are unfulfilled.

Share His Will as yours, and you share what He knows.

If you are God's Will and do not accept His Will, you are denying joy.

Grace is your natural environment.

Being is known by sharing.

CHAPTER 8

The Journey Back

The condition for knowledge is peace.

There is a curriculum of the Atonement.

Your will and God's are one. The Holy Spirit's direction is freedom.

Ask for light and learn that you are light.

Know thyself. When with a brother, you learn what you are because you are teaching him.

Giving of yourself is the function He gave you.

All things are possible through our joint decision.

Freedom is the only gift that you can offer to God's sons.

The undivided will of the Sonship is the perfect creator.

Ask to know the Will of God for you.

Your function is to add to God's treasure.

God has joined all His sons with Himself.

Communication ends separation.

Use your body to communicate truth for the Holy Spirit.

Healing results from using your body for communication.

Health and joy are the unified purpose of God.

Sickness is a strong witness on behalf of
the ego's view of the body as the end.

The ego confuses the means and the end.

The ego has no being and does not know anything.

Ask the Holy Spirit for the right perception of the body.

All healing replaces fear with love.

If you are sick, you are withdrawing from both God and yourself.

Sickness is a sign that the mind is split.

The Holy Spirit's only way of healing is the unification of purpose.

CHAPTER 9

The Acceptance of the Atonement

You need the Holy Spirit as a guide to remind you what you want.

Your will is your salvation, because it is the same as God's.

God is Love, and you do want Him;
ask and you will be answered.

Distort reality and you will be anxious, depressed, and panicky.

The message that your brother gives you is up to you.

Ask the Holy Spirit by giving to Him where you recognize him.

Your task is to tell your brother that he is right, because he is a Son of God.

The one way to handle all errors:
give them to the Holy Spirit to be undone.

The Atonement comes from love.

The arrogance of the ego makes you believe that you can correct your brother.
Correction is of God.

Your identity is shared with your brother, and its sharing is its reality.
This is the lesson of the Atonement.

The Holy Spirit's function is to teach forgiveness.

The Second Coming is the awareness of reality (not its return).

There is light because you see it, but you do not find it by analyzing darkness.

The Holy Spirit's function is as a Guide.

Your brothers are part of you; God knows you as one.

Like God, you are "always."

The ego is also in your mind, because you have accepted it.
The ego attacks you.

Return your part of God and He will give you all.

You can bless others because your grandeur is your abundance.

Love is returned; pride is not.

CHAPTER 10

The Idols of Sickness

God has not changed His Mind about you.

Love your creations as yourself; they are part of you.

Offer the Holy Spirit only your willingness to remember God.

You have His power to heal and comfort your brothers.

To attack the divinity of your brothers is to lose sight of your own.

Place honor at the altar of God and you will find peace.

To know reality, be willing to judge unreality.

Perceiving the spark will heal; knowing the light will create.

Denial of God, of the spark, brings depression, sin, and pain.

Acknowledgment of God is healing.

God has given you the means; listen and remember.

CHAPTER 11

God or the Ego

The closer you come to God, the clearer the light becomes.

Without you, there would be an empty place in God's Mind.

Ask Him what God's Will is for you. He will tell you.
To believe that God's Will is not yours causes sickness and fear.
Be willing for wholeness and, thus, for healing.

God is very quiet, for there is no conflict in Him.

Walk in the light and deny the dark companions.
Only you can darken your own mind.
Blame your brothers, blame yourself; only the ego blames at all.
Dispel illusions by looking at them; they are not dangerous.

Yours is the independence of creation with God.

Establish your autonomy by identifying with God.

Every brother you meet becomes what you perceive in him.

God is leading you to a new kind of experience; do not deny it.

The God of Resurrection demands nothing,
only for you to learn your will and to follow it.

The Call to awake is within you.

Perceptions are variable because the ego confuses illusion and reality.

You have a Teacher; ask Him for what is your truth.

Ask for the real world of freedom.

Accept His healing power and use it.

Exchange your fears for truth and peace.

CHAPTER 12

The Holy Spirit's Curriculum

Every loving thought is true.

Do not deny a brother's call for help.

Fear is an appeal for help, love, and healing.

God cannot be remembered alone.

Look at what you fear.
Help is here. Learn to be quiet in the midst of turmoil.

Learn how to offer the Holy Spirit everything that you do not want.

Those who attack are poor.
Their poverty asks for gifts. Their poverty is not yours.

Any response other than love arises from the ego.
In denying your brother, you deny yourself.

Hatred is in your own mind;
bring your perceptions of the world to Christ at the altar of God.

You cannot be defeated with the guidance of the Holy Spirit.

By guiding your brothers home, you are following Him.

**You have learning handicaps;
the Holy Spirit as Teacher can transcend your limited resources.**

Resign now as your own teacher. You need offer only undivided attention to your Teacher.

You cannot lose—or sell—your soul.

Christ waits for you in perfect peace. Heaven is your home.

Your function is creating and healing.

Look inside for a Guide; look outside for witnesses. Seek and ye shall find.

Your mission is extending peace.

Love is sharing.

The memory of God can dawn only in a mind without the insane desire to control reality.

God gives you the real world in exchange
for the unreal world of despair that you made.

The Atonement is the way back to what was never lost.

CHAPTER 13

The Guiltless World

Love does not kill to save.

You are not guiltless in time, but in eternity.

When you accept the Atonement for yourself, you realize there is no guilt.

There is no journey but only an awakening.

The ego teaches you to attack yourself because you are guilty.

The Atonement is the release from guilt.

Your guilty secret is nothing; the Light will dispel it.

You are more afraid of God than of ego,
and love cannot enter where it is not welcome.

Do not hide suffering from His sight but bring it gladly to Him.

Hell and oblivion are ideas that you made up.

The ego makes the future like the past and thus avoids the present.

The Holy Spirit regards time as temporary, serving a teaching function.

Again and again, you attacked your brother. Love cannot abide in a world apart.

Do not seek vision through your eyes; Christ's vision comes from love.

The Holy Spirit is the Light in which Christ stands revealed.

The miracle enables you to see your brother without his past; truth lies only in the present.

Love always leads to love.

Deny the world you see, for it is costing you another kind of vision.

Exchange your world for the real world and love.

Love waits on welcome, not on time.

Leave your needs to the Holy Spirit.

Quietness is the gift of God.

The Holy Spirit is a thought of God.

Christ's vision is His gift to you; offer it to everyone and everywhere.

To attain freedom, give it to your brother.

Do not be afraid to look within you for the holy sign
of perfect faith your Father has in you.

When you seek to lay guilt on your brother, you will feel guilty.

The end of guilt will never come as long as you believe there is a reason for it.

Love is not special. Love all God's sons equally, as God loves.

The enemy is not real. Heaven is unambiguous.

God gave the Holy Spirit to you with the mission
to remove all doubt and guilt that you have laid upon yourself.

The Holy Spirit offers reconciliation with truth, in which the peace of Heaven lies.

CHAPTER 14

Teaching for Truth

Miracles are a testimony that you are blessed.

You were created only to create.

The Holy Spirit brings the light of truth into the darkness
and lets it shine on you where your brothers see it.

Accept the key to freedom from Christ and join the holy task of bringing light.

You have the power of decision: the alternatives are truth and illusion.

Believe that no one can harm you. What is not of God has no power over you.

**Your every decision is made for the whole Sonship;
ask the Holy Spirit everything.**

He answers with love for everyone touched by a decision.

For your Atonement, grant your brother guiltlessness.

Ask to learn how to forgive.

The guilty and the guiltless cannot communicate.

Each one has a part to play, but the message given to each is the same:
God's Son is guiltless.

From everyone you release from guilt, you learn of your own innocence.
The circle of Atonement is endless.

Holiness must be shared.

Death yields to life; light shines guilt away.

The function of the Holy Spirit is communication.

Perception is the medium that brings ignorance to knowledge.

Bring to the Holy Spirit your secret darkness.

No altar stands to God without His Son.
All is safe within you where the Holy Spirit shines.

Heaven is the union with all of creation.

The Atonement does not make you holy; you were created holy.

The reflection of God shining in you is the power of healing that
you can bring to all the world.

Reach out of time and touch eternity with the help of its reflection in you.

That you can bring order from chaos shows that you are not an ego.

You are too bound to form and not to content.

This course teaches you your identity, and that it is shared.

**One test to recognize truth:
if you are wholly free of fear and if you share in your perfect peace.**

Miracles are for you, every fear or pain undone.

God's Son is indivisible. We are held as one in God.

Make Way For Peace And It Will Come.

CHAPTER 15

The Holy Instant

The Holy Spirit is not bound by time.

The Holy Spirit teaches that there is no hell.

There is no fear in the present when each instant stands clear
from the past and future.

Share the holy instant with your brother.

Offer the holy instant to the Holy Spirit.

The Atonement holds remembrance of God and cannot be bound by time;
it is eternal.

Practice the holy instant;
it is the practice of the power of God in you.

Your every decision represents the value you put on yourself.

Decide for God and invite joy.

Learn to accept what you are but not for yourself alone.

Claim the holy instant anytime and anywhere.

Be willing to let hidden thoughts go.

Without the ego, all would be love.

Because of guilt, all special relationships have elements of fear in them.
In the holy instant, no one is special.

Christ is the Self that the Sonship shares.

God is an idea strengthened by sharing;
in the holy instant, you recognize the idea of love in you.

Lift the veil of time, experience the holy instant.

Ego establishes relationships on guilt.

For the ego, forgiveness becomes impossible.

Forgiveness lies in the communication of minds.

Forgiveness is not your loss but your salvation.

The Holy Spirit deals with your communication problem.

Communication is the only means to establish real relationships.

But, because you have the power, you can turn away from love.

What is not love is always fear.

Choose between total freedom and total bondage.

God asks you for no sacrifice.

Love is where minds are joined without the body's interference.

Communication re-establishes peace and love.

CHAPTER 16

The Forgiveness of Illusions

Sit quietly and let the Holy Spirit relate, empathize, and heal.

Let Him offer His strength to be shared through you.

God recognizes the whole in every part and the part as whole.

Honor the truth, even though you do not understand it.

Do not deny what God has given you.

The Holy Spirit is God's answer to separation.

If you hold God and also all those whom He holds, together you are the universe; for what is beyond God?

Do not barricade hatred with the illusion of love.

Your task is to find all the barricades within you.

Your willingness and His joy make the Holy Spirit a bridge to union.

To make someone guilty is an attack against God.

In a special relationship, one sacrifices the self and trades it for another.

Love is the content and not the form.

Separation is a decision not to know yourself.

Love is freedom; do not place yourself in bondage.

Use time on behalf of reality.

There is a place where Heaven, truth, and beauty wait for you.

The Holy Spirit's task is to atone for your unwillingness by His faith.

Do not seek to lay blame on the past, for it is gone.

Choose between the real Atonement that would heal
and the ego's atonement that would destroy.

The stillness and peace of *now* enfold you in perfect gentleness.

Seek and find His message in the holy instant.

CHAPTER 17

Forgiveness and the Holy Relationship

Give back to God what you reserve for yourself.

Placing ideas aside from truth establishes your prison.

By your own forgiveness, you are free to see.

Salvation gives you the real world of beauty and forgiveness.

Loving thoughts are the spark of beauty in a relationship.

Atonement centers on the past,
which is the source of separation, and where it must be undone.

The past becomes justification for an unholy alliance with ego;
the present allows forgiveness.

The function of the relationship God established with you
became forever "to make happy."

The Holy Spirit has never been separate from anyone.

Accepting ego's gift of death threatens truth with destruction.

Look at the picture and not at the frame.

Offer the relationship to the Holy Spirit.

Only a radical shift in purpose could induce a complete change of mind about what the relationship is for.

God blesses your holy relationship; all it needs now is your blessing.

Maintain, with your brother, your awareness of the holy instant of truth.

Clarify your goal in advance to find the means.

There is no problem that faith will not solve.

A little faithlessness can make your great power useless.

Let truth enter and it will secure the faith you need for peace.

Truth is your goal; salvation of the Son of God is your purpose.

CHAPTER 18

The Passing of the Dream

FEAR: Fragmented Emotion Against Reality.

Look inward for sanity; insanity is outside you.

Your reality is God's creation. Love your brother. He loves you both.

The functions of your holy relationship with your brother are healing and uniting.

The Holy Spirit changes your dreams of fear to happy dreams.

God cannot destroy Himself; His light is in you and darkness cannot put it out.

Your gift of faith offered to your brother was received by God.

Your function is to bring your darkness to light and then bring light back to darkness.

Concentrate on your little willingness;
it will be combined with the power of God's Will.

You need understand nothing.

On your little faith and God's understanding, He will build your part in the Atonement.

God will provide the means to anyone who shares His purpose.

Whatever threatens the peace of one is an equal threat to the other.

God gives knowledge of Himself, an awareness of oneness.

God cannot enter an abode that harbours hate.

You are surrounded only by God;
when you become aware, you gain a sense of liberation, love and peace.

At that Holy Instant, you are released from the past and future and from the body.

It is difficult to reach Atonement by fighting against sin or by meditation.

A holy relationship is a means of saving time, made for you by God.

Be aware of your quiet center; it gives directions.

Call on Love to enter.

Find and welcome brothers; you cannot know God alone.

God would lead you safely through the ring of fear.

The dark clouds of guilt meet forgiveness in the world of light.

A step beyond forgiveness is the source of light.

In that bright world, there is your purpose *now*.

CHAPTER 19

The Attainment of Peace

God heals through you when you set your brother free of the demands of your ego.

The result of an idea is never separate from its source.

Give faith to your brother; give the gift of freedom from the past.

To have faith is to heal.
It is a sign that you have accepted the Atonement and would share it.

Offer grace and blessing to your brother.

Any mistake can be corrected, if truth be left to judge it.

Sin really calls upon love, not fear, and love always answers.

All creation is an extension of God.

To be healed of sin, give it no power over your brother.

The Holy Spirit's purpose extends from you to others with a message.

For peace to spread across Creation, it must begin with you.

Let the Holy Spirit extend the miracle of your relationship to everyone.

When love's messengers are sent, they return with messages of love.

The Holy Spirit gives you love's messengers; they offer you salvation.

The Holy Spirit asks for your pain; He would remove it.

The end of guilt is in your hands to give.

Peace and guilt:
both are conditions of the mind. Your choice.

Equating yourself with the body is an invitation to pain.

Life is the result of the Thought of God.

As you look on your body, so it will seem to be:
corrupted or incorruptible.

Within your newborn purpose lies the end of death.

Give your situation to the Holy Spirit to judge and remove obstacles to your peace.

Answer the Voice of love beyond, and the obstacles to peace disappear.

Give your brother complete forgiveness;
no one reaches love with fear beside him.

Whom you forgive, you free; what you give, you share.

As you look on the giver, so will the gift appear;
the redeemed give joy.

CHAPTER 20

The Vision of Holiness

Honor God by offering your brother lilies (not thorns).

Each gift is an evaluation of the giver and the receiver.

The Holy Spirit's vision is no idle gift.

The new vision looks upon lilies of forgiveness and brings you joy.

The holy look on truth directly and see it within.

The purpose of your holy relationship is happiness and joy for both of you.

Power is God.
It is not up to you to give power.

To each, in seeming solitude, is a savior given.

God gives you your purpose, and also, its fulfillment.

Do not judge what is invisible to you, or you will never see it.

The holy instant is here, right now. Here, then, is everything.

Love does not seek for power, but for relationships.

The Holy Spirit rests within the holy relationship; love shines on it.

You have a real relationship, and it has meaning.

If you want a purpose, you must be willing to want the means.

Salvation is the goal of the Holy Spirit; the means is vision.

Vision is truly given to those who ask to see.

All is redeemed when looked upon with vision.

You can behold the holiness that God gave His Son.

CHAPTER 21

Reason and Perception

How you see the world is a reflection of your inner condition.

Listen, and see if you remember an ancient song.

Light, the vision of the Son of God, is the memory of what you are.

Decide on your goal: sin for suffering or offering to the Holy Spirit for happiness.

Make room for truth. Let it in.

You did not create yourself.

Lack of faith is impossible. Choose where to place your faith.

For vision, look away from sin.

Choose to have faith in the body
only for serving the Holy Spirit's goal as a means for vision.

In a holy relationship, join with what is part of you.

Look within to find the song of freedom. Perception is a choice.

Separate minds influence each other because they are not really separate.

Reason can open doors that you closed against it.

With your brother, you have the power to correct errors.

You are responsible for how your brother sees himself.

Love is given you to give to your brother.

Sin and hatred look for an enemy and they target truth.

Your choice: sin or truth, attack or heal.

Joy cannot be perceived except through constant vision. Wish for constancy.

You need ask for happiness only once, as it is a constant.

CHAPTER 22

Salvation and the Holy Relationship

The sin of the lonely is the desire to rob another to complete himself.

God does not lead you through misery.

The emotion of secrecy opposes love and keeps you blind.

Where fear is powerless, love enters thankfully.

To escape misery, recognize it and go the other way.

You have the means to accomplish the Holy Spirit's purpose: escape from guilt.

To share Christ's vision, be willing to see your brother sinless.

Reason can see the difference between sin and mistakes.

Beyond your brother's errors are his holiness and your salvation.

The first steps along the right way seem hard.

Let illusions be lifted and carry the message of hope and freedom.

God holds your hands as you and your brother stand together.

Everyone yearns for freedom and tries to find it.

The holy relationship is the means of peace.

Each little gift that you offer to your brother lights up the world.

Let truth decide if you be different or the same.

CHAPTER 23

The War Against Yourself

Innocence is strong. Sin of any kind is weakness.

The world is in bitter need of the redemption bestowed by your innocence.

Illusions battle with themselves, but truth is indivisible.

Beloved of Him, you are no illusion.
Let forgiveness sweep away sin.

Laws of chaos attack the truth and govern nothing.

The ego will not enable you to find escape.

Love is the secret ingredient that gives meaning to your life.

You cannot seek to do harm and be saved.

Laws of chaos are illusions;
they have form, but look for the content.

An awareness of peace shows the way to Heaven (ask a friend).

Withhold forgiveness from your brother, and you attack him.

Peace lies within;
any attack to defend it brings murder and guilt.

Be lifted up.
Your purpose is to overlook the battleground.

Conquest is senseless.
Share God's purpose, upheld by His love.

CHAPTER 24

The Goal of Specialness

Your decisions come from your beliefs:
question them.

Realize you journey with your brother.

What you keep from your brother is lost to you.

Sin arises from the idea of specialness.

God has not lost the power to forgive you.

What God has given your brother makes you complete.

Illusions of specialness do not move the truth.

Forgive God for your illusions that He did not give you.

Miracles are merely a change of purpose from hurt to healing.

Christ is at peace because He sees no sin.

The Christ in you is very still.

Christ will exchange His certainty for all your doubts.

The sin you see in your brother keeps you both in Hell.

The Christ in you can see your brother truly.

Out of God's lack of conflict comes your peace.

The test for everything is: What is it for?

God is a means as well as an end.
In Heaven, means and end are one.

Use perception to witness His love.

CHAPTER 25

The Justice of God

You cannot be apart from what is the very center of your life.

See your brother as yourself—join as one in truth.

What is one cannot have separate parts.

The Creator's masterpiece is framed by the Holy Spirit.

Your only function is to behold in your brother the Christ he does not see. Forgive your brother.

Perception: you see what you believe is there.

Heaven's help is within, awaiting our choice. We are not alone.

In you is a vision of joy, gentleness and light for you to extend to others.

Those who offer peace find a home in Heaven—in you is all Heaven.

Forgiven by you, your Savior offers you salvation.

The wish to see calls down the Grace of God upon your eyes.

All that you made can serve salvation easily and well.

What makes no sense and has no meaning is insanity.

The Holy Spirit has the power to change the whole foundation of the world.

Salvation is rebirth of the idea that no one can lose for anyone to gain.

The Holy Spirit cannot use what you withhold.
Only a little faith is asked of you.

The laws of sin demand a victim; this is not justice but insanity.

The innocent who ask for punishment cannot be punished;
justice sets them free.

You have the right to the Universe, as God appointed for His holy Son.

An answer that demands the slightest loss to anyone has not resolved the problem.

Miracles depend on justice. Justice means that no one can lose.

Only forgiveness offers miracles. Take forgiveness for yourself.

What is God's belongs to everyone and is his due.

CHAPTER 26

The Transition

The central theme of attack is that someone must lose.

Merely ask to see a purpose in the world that makes it meaningful.

Your special function is to open the door. The Holy Spirit's function is to release you.

Ask no sacrifice of your brother, so that he does not suffer loss.

There is a borderland between the world and Heaven where illusions meet truth.

There is no sacrifice to give up an illusion for the truth.

Forgiveness turns the world of sin into a world of glory.

Miracles are all the same.

Forget the time of terror that has been so long ago corrected and undone.

Forgive the past and let it go. Look gently on your brother.

All sickness comes from separation and sin.

Perception is a wish and an illusion. Truth is unchanged. God's Will is one.

Salvation asks only for a little wish for Heaven and for truth.

Creation's Law:
Each idea the mind conceives adds to its abundance, never takes away.

A miracle is the little gift of truth already in your memory.

Salvation is immediate: you and your brother become as one.

Look to be delivered, not from time but from the little space between you.

A shadow between your brother and yourself obscures Christ, God and His angels.

Angels hover where an ancient hatred has become a present love.

Beware the temptation to perceive yourself as unfairly treated.

The world is fair because the Holy Spirit has brought injustice to the light within.

CHAPTER 27

The Healing of the Dream

Walk you the gentle way but place no terror symbols on your path.

The strongest witness to futility is sickness.

The Holy Spirit removes blame from the body
and frees the mind to remember Heaven.

Real forgiveness brings a healing to your brother and yourself.

The Law of Miracles obeys love.
Your healing results from showing your brother to be guiltless.

**The Holy Spirit gives you and your brother a shared function:
to correct your mistakes.**

Power used for opposition weakens itself and becomes limited.

True undoing must be kind. Forgiveness is a learning aid.

In quietness are all things answered.

An honest answer asks no sacrifice.

Just one instant of your love without attack allows the miracle of healing.

What is there to fear? Being blessed, you will bring blessing.

Peace is given you when you accept the healing for yourself.

Sin's message is that you are your body, and the cost of pleasure is pain.

To God, sin, pain and death are a single call for healing.

The purpose of the miracle is to accomplish healing.

The first attack upon yourself began when you became separated from your brother.

Awaken and forget all thoughts of death.

The Holy Spirit brings forgiving dreams to replace your nightmares.

The body is the central figure in dreaming of the world.

How willing are you to escape effects of all the world's dreams?

The Holy Spirit bids you bring each terrible effect to Him.
You may laugh together at the foolish cause.

Salvation is a secret you have kept but from yourself.

CHAPTER 28

The Undoing of Fear

The Holy Spirit can make use of memory, not of the past, only of a present state.

When ancient memories of hate appear, remember that their cause is gone.

The miracle comes quietly into the mind that stops an instant and is still.

The Father is a father by His Son.
Fatherhood is creation; the circle of creation has no end.

The cause of healing is the only cause of everything.

Choose forgiving dreams.

**The lesson of the Holy Spirit:
The world is neutral and bodies that seem separate need not be feared.**

Uniting with a brother's mind prevents the cause of sickness.

God bridges the gap of separation,
only if the space is left free of guilt by the miracle.

Find yourself by refusing dreams of sickness and death.
Let your world be lit by miracles.

The Holy Spirit is in your mind and in your brother's.
There is no gap that separates His oneness.

The Holy Spirit takes the broken picture of the Son of God and puts pieces into place;
each piece has His identity.

If you share an evil dream, you will believe that you are the dream and deny yourself.

The gap between you is filled with foggy illusions of sin that are unreal.

Sickness is anger taken out upon the body
in agreement with another's wish for separation.

God promises that there is no gap between Himself and His Sons.

Your home is built upon your brother's health.

God promises His Son safety.

CHAPTER 29

The Awakening

You have a cautious friendship with your brother
because you decided that he is your enemy.

You use your body as an excuse to maintain the gap, for fear of love.

Pain, sin, hate, fear, attack, and guilt: all are one illusion.

He who entered in waits for you to find His gifts of peace and joy.

God is the sum of everything. What is not in Him does not exist.

Make way for love.
You did not create it, but you can extend it by forgiving your brother.

When you are angry,
it is because someone failed to fill the function you allotted him.

Every thought of love you offer the Holy Spirit
brings you nearer to wakening to eternal peace.

Holding in your mind any thought that God did not give you has a great cost.

All goals are set in time, except forgiveness, which is timeless and brings joy.

Seek not outside yourself.

Look not to idols.
God dwells within, and your completion lies in Him.

Salvation seeks to prove that there is no death.

The miracle merely lifts the veil and lets the truth shine.

God has not many sons, but only one. So, who can be given more and who less?

Judge not.
He who judges has need of idols, which are like dangerous toys in a dream world.

Forgiveness brings timelessness so close that the song of Heaven can be heard.

Forgiveness releases one from fear of the judgment brought on by judgment.

CHAPTER 30

The New Beginning

Choose not to judge situations and not to judge what to do.

Reflect quietly. What kind of day do you want?

Don't decide by yourself. Sit by and ask to have the answer given to you.

If you don't like how you feel, it could be that you are wrong about something.

Look for another way of looking at things.

**You cannot make decisions by yourself:
they are made with idols or with God. It's a choice.**

Hear God's perfect Answer.
God joins with you in willing you to be free.

Decide for idols, and you are lost.
Decide for truth, and everything is yours.

The Thought God holds of you is like a star.
He waits for welcome and remembering.

You can be aware of only one reality:
an idol or the Thought God holds of you.

Attack has the power to make illusions seem real.
Illusions must be neither cherished nor attacked.

Salvation asks only that forgiveness be substituted for fear.

All things must be first forgiven and then understood.

An ancient hate is passing from the world.

* A pardon is not justified if it means you sacrifice your rights. *

**Proof of idolatry:
A belief that there are some forms of sickness that forgiveness cannot heal.**

To heal is to make whole.
Do not keep any part of your brother outside your willingness to heal.

One meaning, one shared purpose, applies to everything and ends all ideas of sacrifice.

Establish communication with your brother through the Holy Spirit as interpreter.

Because reality is changeless, a miracle is there to heal all things that change.

See the changeless Christ in your brother and in yourself.
Request a miracle.

CHAPTER 31

The Final Vision

The world was made by the power of your learning skill.

Which lesson will you learn?
The world of guilt and fear? Or the love and hope of God?

When you hear the call to life, give your answer.
He will appear and you will recognize the God of love.

Be innocent of judgment, unaware of any thoughts of evil or good.

Hear the call for life. Be still and listen.

One purpose:
That you and your brother both learn that you love each other, together.

Only if you believe that you deserve attack would you attack anyone.

Learning causes change.
It is only the mind that can learn, not the body.

All the roadways of the world offer no real choice. Seek another way.

To achieve a goal, proceed in its direction.
A journey from yourself does not exist.

The world builds a concept of self for you: an idol with a face of innocence.

The world teaches that you are each a symbol of hidden sins,
so that you will follow the world's laws.

The Holy Spirit helps you look at the evidence and make an active choice.

Seek not yourself in symbols.

As you learn, your concept of yourself changes.

Salvation is the undoing of the world of separation and loss.

God gives you free will to see the world as you will, according to your concept of self.

You cannot see yourself as innocent until one brother sees you worthy of forgiveness.

God allows us the grace to be a savior to brothers entrusted to our care.

The savior's vision sees innocence in everyone and brings them light.

**When God says to you, "Release My Son," listen,
because He is asking for your own release.**

Temptations and trials are lessons. Christ gently says, "Choose again."

Share God's gift of peace with everyone you see, to make the gift your own.

We are one in purpose and the end of hell is near.

The Holy Spirit welcomes all who look to the light
and thanks them for bringing his brothers.

Christ comes to dwell in the abode you set for Him.

**We have reached where all of us are one,
and we are home, where God would have us be.**

Conclusion

Forgiveness, cooperation, empathy and altruism—these are the skills women use to raise a family. Men, on the other hand, tend to compartmentalize these values for family occasions. They sometimes rely on competitive, survival-of-the-fittest, strategizing, and a money-first world view to deal with each other in business and politics. Taken to the extreme, these egocentric, macho values result in car crashes, family feuds, discrimination, and ultimately in war. In fact, they result in death. For His message to reach its target, the channeled Christ speaks to brothers.

This is not to say that women cannot benefit from the *Course*. It is a good tool for them to use against the pressure of society on women to "act like men" in the world of work.

Who is your brother? Anyone and everyone within the sphere of your day—whoever you may come across. That's the challenge presented in *A Course in Miracles*—to treat everyone as a brother with forgiveness, cooperation, and empathy.

The unique thing about the *Course* is that it tells you *how*. With faith only the size of a mustard seed and with willingness to accept the Will of God, you can almost close the gap between you and your brother. The miracle is that God then helps to close the gap the rest of the way. The miracle is that reaching this unity results in love, joy, and peace.

www.ingramcontent.com/pod-product-compliance
Lightning Source LLC
Chambersburg PA
CBHW060457300426
44113CB00016B/2623